Speak LIFE!

WORKBOOK
& JOURNAL

**SHERRY SHEFFIELD &
ROBIN TURNER**

Introduction

We would like to first thank you for deciding to purchase this workbook/ journal. This is the first of many for Sherry and me. We began this book as friends who knew we had great purpose, and this book is one. As Women, Mothers, and Clinicians we understand the impact of mental health and the struggle that comes with talking about it and living with it. It is our hope that this workbook will help you begin the process of exploring and understanding your thoughts and emotions, but also empower you to begin to rewrite the narrative and shift your paradigm, your entire way of seeing yourself and others. Our words have power, and we can begin to take every thought captive and SPEAKLIFE to ourselves. The word of the Lord says, Finally, brethren, whatsoever things are pure, whatsoever things are lovely, whatsoever things are of good report, if they be any virtue, and if there be any praise, think on these things. Philippians 4:8. My prayer is that as you go through the journal portion of the book that you will truly begin to discover the beauty in you!!!!!! Truly see yourself as beautifully and wonderfully made by GOD!! Flaws and ALL!!! As you begin to think and see yourself in a new way, now it is time to speak in a new way. As you journey through this workbook and journal our prayer is that this is the beginning of new life for you. Do not take this journey alone; connect with a friend, family member or Therapist who can come along side you! Be blessed, Sherry and Robin!

Speak
LIFE!

WORKBOOK
— & JOURNAL —

Rejection is felt when we feel like we have been pushed away or not accepted. Rejection can begin as early as childhood or in the loss of a relationship. When we feel rejected by those we care about; we can become isolated or disconnected. To cope with rejection, we must first identify that we feel rejected, and begin to investigate the why we feel this way and where did we first experience the rejection. To heal from rejection, we have known that we are enough right where we are and radically accept ourselves right where we are. When you can accept yourself and know that you are enough; you will begin to draw those people to you who will love and accept you for who you are as well.

Take some time and answer the questions below to identify when you first felt rejected.

1. When did you first feel rejected and why?

_____

_____

_____

_____

_____

_____

_____

_____

2. Who do I need to forgive for making me feel rejected and why do I need to forgive them? Remember to forgive is not about the other person but a release for you!

_____

_____

_____

_____

_____

_____

3. Begin to speak life to that part of you that feels rejected by starting with;

*I AM ENOUGH AND I FULLY ACCEPT _____ ABOUT ME.

What are some things that you need to accept about yourself?

_____

_____

_____

_____

_____

_____

I AM ENOUGH AND I FULLY ACCEPT ME FLAWS AND ALL!!

Abandonment says that I am undesired, left behind and even discarded! it leaves the feeling of being alone or simply by myself. The feeling of abandonment can make us isolate from people and even the world; like there is no one there for me. Because of the feeling we intentionally begin to say things to ourselves like: No one understands me, it must be something about me that people continue to leave me. That is not true! While people may have failed us or even left. We are never alone. To heal from abandonment, we must begin to speak life to that part of ourselves. Really the desire is a longing and truly a desire to be connected to others. To speak life to this part of you; begin to say" I am never alone for the lord has given me a comforter in the holy spirit."

FOR LAST WE SHARE ABUNDANTLY IN THE SUFFERING OF CHRIST, SO ALSO OUR COMFORT ABOUNDS THROUGH CHRIST. 2ND CORITHINANS 1:5 NIV

1. I speak to abandonment and I say_____

_____

_____

_____

_____

_____

_____

Fear can be broken down to ; false, evidence, appearing to be real. This means that I am looking at people, circumstances, and even myself from a distorted perspective. Which begins to cause anxiety, and even leading on to full on panic! attacks. fear says; you are not safe, you cannot trust and you cannot be who you were always meant to be... when living life from a perspective of fear, you know longer have the courage or boldness to love yourself and others because you are afraid to let people in to see you. Fear permits you from stepping out and being creative. you are paralyzed! you can see yourself physically growing and aging, and even going through the motions of life. You have yet to live until you can step out of comfort and be bold and courageous enough to love and create new experiences in life. To heal from fear, you must be honest about what you fear, and why you fear it. Then comes the challenging part... be vulnerable enough to open you heart again to the unknown of love, creativity, risk, and jump into life!

FEAR IS LIKE A SEED IN THAT HAS BEEN PLANTED IN THE HEART AND HAS BEGUN TO TAKE ROOT.

1. Identify where fear began for you?

_____

_____

_____

_____

_____

2. How has fear been impacting your choices/decisions?

_____

_____

_____

_____

_____

_____

_____

3. What has your fear held you back from?

_____

_____

_____

_____

_____

_____

_____

4. Speak life to the area of your life in which you know fear has impacted you..

I say to fear _____

_____

_____

_____

_____

_____

_____

_____

_____

5. In releasing fear; I choose to see myself as...

_____

_____

_____

_____

_____

_____

_____

_____

I AM BOLD AND I AM COURAGEOUS!

FOR GOD HAS NOT GIVEN US A SPIRIT OF FEAR BUT OF POWER LOVE AND A SOUND MIND.

2ND TIMOTHY 1:7

Anxiety and worry are fear-based emotions. Worry is the constant unease and racing of the mind about life, and circumstances. Worry is like ruminating thoughts that are a tap playing over and over in your mind. It is like attempting to have control over the things that you have no control of. Constant worry breathes anxiety. Anxiety creates restlessness and trouble with focus and concentration. To begin the healing of anxiety is to learn to let go of what is out of your control and do what is within our control. Be at peace with what is.

I AM NOT SAYING THIS BECAUSE I AM IN NEED, FOR I HAVE LEARNED TO BE CONTENT WITH WHATEVER THE CIRCUMSTANCES. VS.12 I KNOW WHAT IT IS TO BE IN NEED, AND I KNOW WHAT IT IS TO HAVE PLENTY. I HAVE LEARBNED THE SECRET OF BEING CONTENT IN ANY AND EVERY SITUATION, WHETHER WELL FED OR HUNGRY, WHETHER LIVING IN PLENTY OR IN WANT. VS. 13 I CAN DO ALL THIS IN CHRIST WHO GIVES ME STRENGTH. PHILLIPPIANS 4:11-14

Learning to let go and let God is not always an easy thing. but today to have peace what can you begin to let go and give to God?

Worry is a behavior that could have been learned

1. How did you learn to worry?

_____

_____

_____

_____

2. I say to worry; I will no longer hold on to....

_____

_____

_____

_____

_____

_____

3. To truly release the behavior of worry. What can you release to God and believe him to do?

_____

_____

_____

_____

_____

_____

4. When you begin to feel yourself begin to worry and you have released the circumstance, and situation to God. What are some other things that you can do to help you in this area to begin walking in faith?

_____

_____

_____

_____

_____

_____

5. What does walking by faith and not by sight mean to you?

_____

_____

_____

_____

_____

BE ANXIOUS FOR NOTHING, BUT IN EVERYTHING BY PRAYER AND SUPPLICANTION, WITH THANKSGIVING LET YOUR REQUEST BE MADE KNOWN TO GOD.

PHILLIPPIANS 4:6

Holding on to the past can stop you from moving forward in life, and in relationships. We are to learn from the past to better ourselves for the future. To hold on to past mistakes means; I do not learn from the mistake. To hold on to past hurt and pain; does not allow you to be emotionally open and available to others. Letting go of the past is not easy or comfortable but necessary for you to become your best self. To let go of the past and begin to heal is to allow yourself to feel the hurt and the pain of the past but to invite compassion for yourself and others. you are not your mistakes, and you are not what others may have done to you.

1. What in your past have you been holding on to?

_____

_____

_____

_____

2. Why has this area of your life been a struggle to let go?

_____

_____

_____

_____

How has holding on to the past impacted your life?

_____

_____

_____

_____

_____

_____

3. If I were to let go of the circumstance or situation; I may experience what in my life.

_____

_____

_____

_____

_____

LET BE, LET GO, AND LET GROW, NEW LIFE!

THEREFORE, IF ANYONE IS IN CHRIST, HE IS A NEW CREATION. THE OLD HAS PASSED AWARY; BEHOLD THE NEW HAS COME.

2ND CORITHINANS 5:7

Unforgiveness is much like holding on to the past. Withholding forgiveness of others does not impact the other person. It mostly impacts you! Unforgiveness is negative energy that is stored in your heart, that begins to harden your heart over time. Unforgiveness can begin to bring other negative emotions such as jealously, envy, bitterness, and resentment. Over time unforgiveness can create isolation from the people you love the most! There times that we need to forgive others and letting them go is still necessary. Even in those moments to choose to forgive is liberating for you and even freeing for the other person. Forgiveness is a decision, that the heart begins to catch up to. Choosing to forgive yourself is also necessary. It is showing compassion for yourself versus punishment of self. Choosing forgiveness toward self and others is one of the most loving acts you can do...

1. Who do you need to forgive and what are you forgiving them for?

2. How has not forgiving them/yourself had an impact on you?

_____

_____

_____

_____

_____

_____

_____

3. What other negative emotions have come up for you because of unforgiveness?

_____

_____

_____

_____

_____

_____

_____

4. What has been the struggle of letting of releasing yourself/ them from this circumstance or situation you have been holding on too?

_____

_____

_____

_____

_____

_____

5. If you were to let go; what will you experience going forward?

_____

_____

_____

_____

_____

_____

I CHOSE TO WALK IN LIBERTY!

BEARING WITH ONE ANOTHER AND, IF ONE HAS A COMPLAINT AGAINST ANOTHER, FORGIVING EACH OTHER; AS THE LORD HAS FORGIVEN YOU, SO MUST ALSO FORGIVE.

Childhood trauma is the leading cause of mental health, and substance abuse disorder. Trauma is not only stored in the mind, but it is also stored in your body. Trauma can be experienced by abuse, neglect, rape, molestation, domestic violence, emotional verbal abuse or crime. Trauma can shift the way we see ourselves and the way we see others and impact the way we connect with others. Trauma can hold you paralyzed in fear if never healed. If you have experienced trauma it is easily to say that speak to this area of your life, but the truth is healing from trauma is a process and takes intentional work! I recommend connecting with a therapist who is trained in trauma focused work.

When healing from trauma you may experience a flood of emotions which is normal. Some of the emotions experienced are remarkably like the stages of grief. You may feel; anger, sadness, bargaining, depression, and then come to the place of acceptance. Acceptance is knowing that the incident occurred, but you are now able to sit in your truth and allow yourself to feel the pain without numbing or avoiding. Knowing that everything you feel is normal and okay. Connect with those that you trust those that will allow you to share you most raw and authentic emotions in a safe space.

When you begin to heal from whatever you may have experienced. You will find that you can begin to share your experience without the same pain and even shame that may have been connected to the incident. Again, when you are ready to really address your trauma it is beneficial to talk with a therapist. A therapist can guide you through each emotion and help you explore each emotion without judgement or shame. A therapist will also assist in helping you to identify healthy coping skills as you move through the process to healing.

Have you experienced trauma that you believe is still impacting your life today?

How has this incident impacted the way that you see yourself?

Has this incident impacted the way you see others and connect with others?

_____

_____

_____

_____

_____

_____

_____

What behaviors do you have now that may be due to the trauma that you have experienced?

_____

_____

_____

_____

_____

_____

_____

What decisions have you made in your life that may be a result of your trauma?

_____

_____

_____

_____

_____

_____

What do you think your life would look like if you allowed yourself to go through the process of healing?

_____

_____

_____

_____

_____

_____

To begin the process of healing what do you feel you need? What steps can you take to begin the process?

_____

_____

_____

_____

_____

_____

_____

Who do you feel that you can call or connect with to support you in the healing process?

_____

_____

_____

_____

_____

_____

_____

In speaking life to yourself. What can you say to keep you encouraged in the healing process when and if it becomes difficult?

_____

_____

_____

_____

_____

_____

_____

Identify a total of 3 therapeutic agencies that you can call to being services when you're ready?

1. _____

2. _____

3. _____

When you think of self-care the first thing that comes to mind is physical health. Eating right and exercise. But self-care also includes taking care of your mental health. Depression and anxiety are on the rise which make it difficult to handle life's day to day responsibilities. Depression makes you feel a loss of interest in the things you would normally enjoy, increase in sleep or lack of sleep. Isolation, and increase or decrease in eating. Physical illness is also something that we do not expect but it happens. To begin the process of mental health it can begin with what we say to ourselves and how we can encourage and motivate ourselves to admit that you need help, and then asking for the help. Mental and physical illness can be treated many ways, but after acknowledging there is something going on in the mind or body. It is important to quiet yourself and ask yourself; what do I need in this moment and how can I begin to meet that need. Who can I talk to and be safe to be transparent, without judgment? Safe places are not always with the people that we expect. Safe places can be a counselor, family member, co-worker, peer, and a least expected friend. I always recommend starting with the father in heaven who can lead you and guide you to who and where you connect. While mental, emotional, and physical healing is a process, know that it is not impossible!! Speak life to your mind, and body!

1. Have you felt depressed or anxious, and when did you begin to experience these feelings _____

_____

_____

_____

2. How is your physical health? Have you felt sick, sluggish, pains, and when did you begin to experience these health problems?

_____

_____

_____

3. When was the last time you saw a doctor?

_____

_____

_____

_____

_____

4. Who can you trust to talk to about what you are feeling? Pick a person that you know loves you without judgement, and can be honest with you, and who you can receive the honesty from.

_____

_____

_____

_____

_____

5. Is there a fear in talking to someone about you're your feeling and why? _____

_____

_____

_____

6. Being to pray and ask the lord to help you in the area of

_____

_____

_____

_____

7. What are some loving words that you can begin to speak over your mind? _____

_____

_____

_____

_____

What are some things that you can begin to do that can help you work on your physical body. Begin with realistic goals that you know you will do. They can be as specific as I am going to make a doctor's appointment today, I am going to add more vegetables in my diet, or I plan to be in bed earlier each night. Often, we start with the huge plans that are difficult to start. Keep the goals small and find someone who you can connect with to help you meet your goals.

8. What is a small goal that you can begin regarding your physical health? _____

_____

_____

_____

_____

_____

What are some loving words that you can speak over your physical health. I don't care what the issue is with your health; we can always speak love and kindness to ourselves to push us to keep going, keep living, and stay encouraged not matter what we may be facing. Our journey of mental and physical health can inspire someone else.

9. I speak to my physical health and I say_____

_____

_____

_____

_____

_____

10. What are some habits that you may need to change in your life?

_____

_____

_____

_____

_____

_____

11. What are some new habits that I can begin in my life?

_____

_____

_____

_____

_____

_____

_____

_____

BUT HE WAS WOUNDED FOR OUR TRANSGRESSIONS, HE WAS BRUISED FOR OUR INIQUITIES; THE CHASTISEMENT FOR OUR PEACE WAS UPON HIM, AND BY HIS STRIPES WE ARE HEALED.

ISAIAH 53

We were all created by GOD and created with a God given purpose. To discover our purpose, we must be intentional about our connection to the Father. He is the one that created us and knows us better then we know ourselves. The word says," Seek first God's Kingdom and: his righteous; and all these things will be added unto you. Matthew 6:33" So, we can seek God even for purpose, and he will provide ALL that we need to accomplish what he has already placed on the inside of us. There are times when fear and doubt attempt to speak to us and say that it is impossible. Even close friends and family can make us doubt what we feel deep on the inside. Faith says," With God ALL things are possible." It is important to speak to our purpose and destiny and give it life. We are to water purpose and destiny with our words, time and attention, and Faith. Faith requires action. Begin by seeking the father..

Lord I seek you and I ask _____

_____

_____

_____

_____

Lord help me to _____

_____

_____

_____

I speak to my purpose and destiny and say _____

_____

_____

_____

_____

_____

To begin moving into purpose and destiny; I can begin to _____

_____

_____

_____

_____

_____

I will know that I am now closer to purpose and destiny when _____

_____

_____

_____

_____

_____

What are the distractions or habits that I need to remove from life to help me focus on my purpose and destiny _____

_____

_____

_____

_____

By faith I speak _____

_____

_____

_____

_____

For I know the plans I have for you, declares the Lord, "plans to prosper you and not to harm you, plans to prosper you and not to harm you, plans to give you hope and a future.

Jeremiah 29:11-13

Life's circumstances and experiences can literally break your heart. Feelings of "I should have done this, and I could have done that." Focusing on the mistakes you made, or the anger and pain of a broken relationship can make us feel literally broken. The feeling that something is missing or a whole in your very heart. If you have been in a relationship that ended, and you can still feel the pain in your heart. This is the feeling of being broken. While all these circumstances make us feel broken; we are in fact still here, and if you can allow yourself the time to heal from every circumstance you will see that you are in fact whole and lacking nothing. You are right where you are supposed to be, and that situation or circumstance was just a temporal experience that allows you the opportunity to grow and mature. You will see the beauty from the ashes. Like it or not; we were meant to go through some of the things we have gone through, we are meant to feel the hurt and pain. It is how we get our joy after mourning, our strength from weakness. It is truly how we can begin again. Begin loving again, hoping again, and began living again. There is in fact love after brokenness.

What experience or circumstance has made you feel broken

_____

_____

_____

_____

_____

_____

What have you lost hope for or in _____

_____

_____

_____

_____

_____

How has the feeling of brokenness impacted your life_____

_____

_____

_____

_____

_____

I AM WHOLE AND LACKING NOTHING!

Healing from brokenness will look like what for you and in your life

_____

_____

_____

_____

Who do I need to work on forgiving to begin the processing of healing

_____

_____

_____

_____

_____

What do I need to let go of in this moment and leave in the past

_____

_____

_____

_____

What does wholeness and lacking nothing look like for me _____

_____

_____

_____

_____

_____

_____

I speak to brokenness and I say _____

_____

_____

_____

_____

_____

_____

Lord I ask you to heal _____

_____

_____

_____

_____

_____

_____

_____

By faith I believe _____

_____

_____

_____

_____

_____

_____

_____

The Lord is near to the broken hearted and saves the crushed *in spirit.*

Psalm 34:18

In life there are times we can experience doubt about who we are and what we are capable of. We can even begin to look at what others are doing and how they are living and only see what we are lacking. Doubt is literally like a seed that can also begin to take root in our hearts, and like any seed it can begin to take root and grow within us. Our body and our minds begin to believe that we are but mere grasshoppers. To overpower the seed of doubt, again we must begin to see the greatness that lies within us. Greatness is that area in our lives that we often see as a hindrance or a weakness, we often try to hide it, but it bursts out every time we are allowing ourselves the freedom to just be our true selves. Greatness shows up every time we are doing the thing that we love to do. Greatness shows up even when we continue to live after the mistakes and trials of life. Greatness shows up when we are doing what we love. Greatness shows up when we can be there for others. Greatness is truly the Glory of God within! Greatness is when we can see what God see's in ourselves!

When does doubt begin to show up in your life _____

_____

_____

_____

_____

_____

_____

What has doubt spoken to you _____

_____

_____

_____

_____

_____

How has doubt impacted your life and your choices _____

_____

_____

_____

_____

_____

I speak to doubt and say that I am _____

_____

_____

_____

_____

_____

I speak to doubt and say that I am capable of _____

_____

_____

_____

_____

I will continue to speak life to myself by saying _____

_____

_____

_____

_____

In this moment I am letting go and leaving behind _____

_____

_____

_____

_____

Much like doubt discouragement can come through disappointments. We can often become discouraged by what we can consider to be failure, and loss in our life. It is feeling that things did not go the way we expected. Discouragement grows and breaths from the expectations that we put on our self and the expectation that we put on others. There are times when we must release expectations that done leave room for humanity. The fact is there are many times in life when things do not go as planned. To feel discouragement is humane, but do not sit it in too long. You must get right back up and try again. Life does not stop because things did not go as we planned, but we can do what is in our control which is to not give and try again. Do not lose heart, and do not lose hope!

I feel discouraged when _____

_____

_____

_____

_____

I release myself from the expectation of _____

_____

_____

_____

_____

_____

I release others from the expectation of _____

_____

_____

_____

_____

What have you given up due to disappointment that you should give
another try _____

_____

_____

_____

_____

Who has specifically disappointed you _____

_____

_____

_____

_____

I speak to discouragement and say _____

_____

_____

_____

_____

I am trusting the Lord with_____

_____

_____

_____

I DARE NOT LOSE HEART!

May the God of hope fill you with all joy and peace as you trust in Him, so that you may overflow with hope by the power of the Holy Spirit.

Romans 15:13

There is a difference between perfectionism and wanting to do things in excellence. Perfectionism holds a standard that does not leave room for mistakes. Perfectionism is really that internal critic that places judgement of oneself for any mistake or not reaching this imaginary line/standard we need to meet placed there by ourselves, society, family, co-workers, peers, and friends. If one is critical of themselves, they are usually over critical of others. Perfectionism says, "I am not enough as I am. I have to do and be better." Perfectionism says," I need to meet everyone else's needs and expectations of who I should be." It says that I am never enough, and even when you do amazing things, and simply be your amazing self, that one thing or one area that you see as a weakness; makes you not enough. Perfectionism can have you living in shame and guilt, and not living at all. I dare you to speak to that place of perfectionism that says you are not enough just as you are. NO really; just as you are!!! You were not made to be, look, or act like anyone else. You were made to be unique, make mistakes, be awkward, goofy, loving, and yes sometimes annoying YOU!! But that is how GOD made you! Love you! Yes, work in a spirit of excellence, give things your 100%, but none of that makes you the beautiful being that you are! LOVE YOURSELF and BE YOURSELF!

1. Do you always feel like you have to be and do things perfectly?

_____

_____

_____

_____

2. When did you begin to first feel perfectionism show up for you?

_____

_____

_____

_____

_____

3. Triggers are people, places, things, situations, or circumstances that can bring uncomfortable emotions such as needing to be perfect or feeling weak and defeated. What triggers perfectionism for you?

_____

_____

_____

_____

_____

4. What are some of the negative things that you have said to yourself about yourself?

_____

_____

_____

_____

5. What are some affirming words that you can say to yourself to replace the negative thoughts about yourself?

_____

_____

_____

_____

_____

6. When you feel like others are critical of you, what can you speak to yourself?

_____

_____

_____

_____

_____

7. Who are you connected to that can see you and love you right where you are?

_____

_____

_____

_____

8. What does self-acceptance look like for you?

_____

_____

_____

_____

_____

9. I speak to perfectionism and say

_____

_____

_____

_____

_____

I AM ENOUGH JUST AS I AM!

Who called us to a holy calling, not because of our works but because of his own purpose and grace, which He gave to us in Christ Jesus before the ages began.

2nd Timothy 1:9

The inability to say no can come from the need to please. This is also known as co-dependency. The excessive emotional or psychological reliance on another. A co-dependent relationship causes one to given into the unhealthy emotional, psychological and behavior of another. For example, a woman's husband cheated on her and he decides that he wants to leave the relationship, and the woman says to him; if you leave me, I will kill myself. I can't live without you." This is an example of a codependent relationship. If you struggle with making decisions and depend on others to tell you if the decision is right or wrong; this is another example of co-dependency. In a co-dependent relationship it is difficult to maintain your own identify.

One of the indicators that you are in a healthy relationship is that you feel safe to be yourself and even make mistakes without fear of abandonment and rejection... You must speak to codependency and say," it's okay to be me." When you do not feel safe to be who you really are in any relationship. Well; I call that a red flag, and that is an unhealthy relationship for you., and it is okay to choose to release yourself from that relationship. Communicating when you don't feel safe in your relationships is very important. Review the i statement below to help you begin to c0mmunicate your thoughts and feelings.

(EXAMPLE OF I STATEMENT BELOW)

I FEEL_____HURT_____WHEN YOU ARE NOT HONEST WITH ME

I WOULD LIKE FOR YOU TO TREAT ME WITH THE SAME RESPECT I GIVE YOU.

IF YOU CAN NOT RESPECT ME; **I FEEL IT IS IN THE BEST INTERST FOR ME TO END THIS REALTIONSHIP.**

I statements are a great way of learning how to communicate your thoughts and feelings/emotions without pointing the finger at others. We are only in control of ourselves and we are unable to control other thoughts, feelings, emotions, and behavior.

If you are in a co-dependent relationship where there is abuse, emotionally, mentally, or physically. Please seek help and a safe place! It is difficult to leave a relationship where there is abuse, and you should have a plan and someone that you can trust that you can call and that will support you if you choose to leave.

Therapeutic treatment is also greatly beneficial when in an abusive relationship.

YOU ARE WORTHY OF LOVE, SUPPORT, AND ENCOURAGEMENT. ABUSE AND VIOLENCE IS NOT A DEMONSTRATION OF LOVE.

Speak to co-dependency and say that I have a voice, and it is okay to say no. Let your yes be yes, and your no be no! If someone leaves because of your no, then the season of that relationship may be up remember to speak life to yourself and say;*I AM WORTHY OF A HEALTHY AND LOVING RELA-TIONSHIP."**

Signs of codependency are as listed;

1. Having difficulty making decisions in a relationship.
2. Having difficulty identifying your own feelings.

3. Having difficulty communicating in a relationship.

4. Valuing the approval of others more than valuing yourself.

5. Low self-esteem

6. No longer trusting your own thoughts and opinions.

7. Fear of abandonment or rejection

You can overcome co-dependency by;

1. Loving and accepting yourself.

2. Forgiving yourself for any mistakes that you may have made in the past.

3. Seeing the beauty in your uniqueness

4. Healing from pass trauma

5. Psychotherapy

6. Connecting with people that love and accept you for who you are

7. Let go of relationships that cause you to question yourself and be overly critical of yourself

Have you struggled with being yourself in certain relationships? With whom do you struggle to be yourself?

_____

_____

_____

_____

Do you struggle with fear of rejection or abandonment? When did you first experience this fear?

_____

_____

_____

_____

_____

Where do you feel the fear or anxiety in your body?

_____

_____

_____

_____

Do you often seek approval in your relationships? What behaviors have you displayed to gain the approval of others?

_____

_____

_____

_____

What do you find as awesome and unique about yourself?

_____

_____

_____

_____

_____

_____

Are there some relationship or friendships that you need to let go of?

_____

_____

_____

_____

If you were to let go of these unhealthy relationships; how do you think your life would change?_____

_____

_____

_____

Who in your life do you feel you can be your most authentic self with? Why do you feel you can be yourself in this relationship? Is this relationship healthy? _____

_____

_____

_____

_____

_____

How would you define your authentic self? _____

_____

_____

_____

_____

_____

As you are becoming more intentional about addressing anything and everything that would attempt you from holding you back from being your authentic self. It is just as important to identify purpose and destiny.

Begin by identifying 3 goals that you would like to accomplish before the end of the year. Identifying goals in life keep you moving forward and on the path of an authentic and purposeful life.

Goal #1

Step #1 to accomplish my goal

Step #2 to accomplish my goal

Step #3 to accomplish my goal

Goal #2

Step# 1 to accomplish my goal

Step # 2 to accomplish my goal

Step # 3 to accomplish my goal

Goal #3

Step #1 to accomplish my goal

Step #2 to accomplish my goal

Step #3 to accomplish my goal

1 CORITHIANS 13:4-13

1 CORINTHIANS 13:4 LOVE IS PATIENT , LOVE IS KIND. IT DOES NOT ENVY, IT DOES NOT BOAST. IT IS NOT PROUD. IT DOES NOT DISHONOR OTHERS. IT IS NOT SELF-SEEKING. IT IS NOT EASILY ANGERED. IT KEEPS NO RECORD OF WRONGS. LOVE DOES NOT DELIGHT IN EVIL BUT REJOICES WITH THE TRUTH. IT ALWAYS PROTECTS, ALWAYS TRUSTS, ALWAYS HOPES AND ALWAYS PERSERVERS. LOVE NEVER FAILS. BUT WHERE THERE ARE PROPHECIES, THEY WILL CEASE, WHERE THERA ARE TONGUES, THEY WILL BE STILLED, WHERE THERE IS KNOWLEDGE, IT WILL PASS AWAY. FOR WE KNOW IN PART AND PROPHESY IN PART. BUT WHEN COMPLETENESS COMES, WHAT IS IN PART DISAPPEARS.

WHEN I WAS A CHILD, I TALKED LIKE A CHILD. I THOUGHT LIKE A CHILD, I REASONED LIKE A CHILD. WHEN I BECAME A MAN, I PUT THE WAYS OF CHILDHOOD BEHIND ME. FOR NOW WE SEE ONLY A REFLECTION AS IN A MIRROR, THEN WE SHALL SEE FACE TO FACE. NOW I KNOW IN PART, THEN I SHALL KNOW FULLY, EVNE AS I AM FULLY KNOWN. AND NOW THESE THREE REMAIN, FAITH, HOPE, AND LOVE. BUT THE GREATEST OF THESE IS LOVE!

Dedication

This journal is dedicated first and foremost to the Lord Jesus Christ who orchestrated the union of two beautiful caring women who became great friends and sisters in Christ.

To the men and women who have suffered from trauma may this book be the guide to healing your soul through the empowerment of speaking life!

-God bless-

From: Sherry Sheffield, MA, LPC, LADC & Robin Turner, MS, LMFT-I, CADC-I

Acknowledgements

To my partner, colleague, d-9 sister, and sister in Christ; thank you for being an anointed spirit, guide, and friend who continues to push and encourage me to speak life and love myself! You are truly a virtuous woman robin turner and it is a pleasure to be in your presence! May our friendship continue to grow!

To my husband and children, thank you for being supportive of me as i spent hours away doing god's work. You all are the backbone of my life and success!

And finally, I give thanks to my life, all the trials and tribulations, tears, fears, ups & downs! Thank you for teaching me the lessons needed to pour into every soul who picks up this journal! I will continue to speak life and be open to the change!

-Sherry Sheffield, MA, LPC, LADC

This journal belongs to:

Remember you are blessed, beautiful, & loved just the way you are! Get ready to speak life! Enjoy the journey and trust the process one day and one step at a time!

It is easy to dwell on what you do not have and your shortcomings; challenge yourself to name 5 things that are going well for you and 5 positive attributes about yourself.

The things that are going well in my life right now are:

1. _____

_____

_____

_____

_____

2. _____

_____

_____

_____

_____

3. _____

_____

_____

4. _____

5. _____

My positive attributes are:

1. _____

_____

_____

_____

_____

2. _____

_____

_____

_____

_____

3. _____

_____

_____

_____

_____

4. _____

_____

_____

_____

_____

_____

5. _____

_____

_____

_____

_____

_____

One act of kindness leads to a domino effect of goodness in the world. What have you done for someone lately?

My personal goals:

1. _____

_____

_____

_____

2. _____

_____

_____

_____

_____

3. _____

_____

_____

_____

_____

My family goals:

1. _____

_____

_____

_____

_____

2. _____

_____

_____

_____

_____

3. _____

_____

_____

_____

_____

My community goals:

1. _____

_____

_____

_____

_____

2. _____

_____

_____

_____

_____

_____

3. _____

_____

_____

_____

_____

_____

My purpose is:

(Take this time and meditate on what god has called you to do; think about things you are passionate about and your natural talents)

_____

_____

_____

_____

_____

_____

_____

_____

_____

_____

_____

_____

_____

My _____ is beautiful.

(Look at yourself in the mirror and think about who you are as a person; what do you find the most beautiful about you and why?)

Isn't it a beautiful thing that you woke up this morning? What a blessing it is! *Take some time and think about this statement and fill in the blank:*

Every morning when I rise, I make it a duty to ...

We all serve a purpose in life both men and women; however, it is important to be in tuned with yourself mind, body, and spirit. Take this moment to complete this statement:

As a (man/woman) I feel as if I must be more in tune with...(WHY?)

_____

_____

_____

_____

_____

_____

_____

_____

_____

_____

_____

_____

_____

Replenish yourself daily so that you can practice the art of companion and cultivate a deeper sense of love towards yourself and others.

I will replenish myself by doing the following:

1. _____

_____

_____

_____

_____

2. _____

_____

_____

_____

_____

3. _____

_____

_____

_____

4.

5.

By doing these things, it will allow me to:

_____

_____

_____

_____

_____

_____

_____

_____

_____

_____

_____

_____

_____

_____

_____

_____

Many times, in life we become turned around, twisted, and confused when things become overwhelmed; despite these events it is important to remember who you are. Take some time to answer this question and go beyond the titles and labels that are placed on you in your everyday life.

Who am I?

Radical Acceptance means to accept your reality whatever it is whole heartedly. This does not mean you condone any wrongdoing that has happened to you or agree with the outcome. When you choose to accept your reality, you can then begin to heal through forgiveness. Remember, forgiveness is not for the other person it is for you.

Ask yourself who or what do you need to forgive to move forward with your life?

What are your insecurities? Know that these are lies and barriers keeping you from your purpose, desires, and destiny in life.

My insecurities are:

1. _____

_____

_____

_____

_____

2. _____

_____

_____

_____

_____

3. _____

_____

_____

_____

4. _____

_____

_____

_____

These are things i will do to overcome the insecurities:

1. _____

_____

_____

_____

2. _____

_____

_____

3.

4.

Gratitude for me is... Remember being thankful for what you have now allows for doors to be open in the future.

I am thankful for:

1. _____

_____

_____

_____

_____

2. _____

_____

_____

_____

_____

3. _____

_____

_____

_____

4. _____

_____

_____

_____

_____

_____

5. _____

_____

_____

_____

_____

_____

6. _____

_____

_____

_____

_____

_____

The reason I am thankful for these things are:

_____

_____

_____

_____

_____

_____

_____

_____

_____

_____

_____

_____

_____

_____

_____

_____

_____

_____

_____

Everyday courage is having the ability to speak your truth and know that you are good enough. What is your truth?

My truth is:

Remember that you are accepted and loved by god first; therefore, accepting and loving yourself is important as this will allow you to teach people how you need to be treated. Currently think about what you need to accept and love about yourself:

I fully accept the following about myself:

1. _____

_____

_____

_____

_____

2. _____

_____

_____

_____

_____

3. _____

_____

_____

4. _____

_____

_____

_____

_____

5. _____

_____

_____

_____

_____

These are things I love about me:

1. _____

_____

_____

_____

_____

2. _____

_____

_____

_____

_____

3. _____

_____

_____

_____

_____

4. _____

_____

_____

_____

_____

5. _____

_____

_____

_____

_____

In accepting and loving myself, i am teaching others what?

_____

_____

_____

_____

_____

_____

_____

_____

_____

There is a difference with being alone and being lonely. You must learn to be comfortable with being alone with yourself but also know that you are never alone because the lord has given you a comforter in his holy spirit. Name ways you can learn to be comfortable with being alone and explore what you can do with this time.

When I am alone, I can:

_____

_____

_____

_____

_____

_____

_____

_____

_____

_____

_____

_____

_____

This will teach me:

_____

_____

_____

_____

_____

_____

_____

_____

_____

_____

_____

_____

_____

_____

_____

_____

_____

Anger is a surface emotion that masks a core emotion such as hurt, resentment, pain, or even embarrassment. Understanding and daring to explore your emotions are important to the healing process. Take some time to explore what you are healed from because you no longer need anger to defend you from your hurt and pain.

Today, I am healed from:

This means what for my life:

_____

_____

_____

_____

_____

_____

_____

_____

_____

_____

_____

_____

_____

_____

_____

_____

_____

Be encouraged and know that the power of life lies in your tongue. Never lose heart and always trust in the Lord! Today write about faith!

By faith I am:

_____

_____

_____

_____

_____

_____

_____

_____

_____

_____

_____

_____

_____

We have all been subject to our own criticism making us our own worst critic and distorting the perspective of one's self. Today speak to your inner and external critics by completing this exercise.

I am more than capable of:

_____

_____

_____

_____

_____

_____

_____

_____

_____

_____

_____

REMEMBER YOU CAN DO ALL THINGS THROUGH CHRIST WHO STRENGTHENS YOU!

Perfectionism is a distorted thought pattern that leads to feelings of being inadequate and a less than. Simply put, it takes away from the true you! Know that you are perfectly imperfect and have been given the grace to just be you! Complete the following sentence.

I no longer must be perfect at:

_____

_____

_____

_____

_____

_____

_____

_____

_____

_____

Free writing day: Take this day to freely write wat is on your heart and soul!

Today's word is LOVE! What does this word mean to you? How do you know that you are being loved? What are you doing to love yourself?

Free writing day: Take this day to freely write what is on your heart and soul!

Today's word is DETERMINATION. What are you determined to accomplish today that will prepare you for your tomorrow?

Today's words are MIND, BODY, and SPIRIT! How will you take care of your mind today? What will you do to nourish your body? Have you been spiritually fed?

Question of the day: What does speak life mean to you? How have you begun to speak positivity into your life and what has changed?

Today's activity is titled: "A Song in My Heart." Examine your life and create an album with titles that outline important times in your life! Do not forget to name the album itself. Once you are finished write down why you chose the name for your album and what are favorite tracks as well as your least favorites.

TRACKS 1 _____

_____

2 _____

_____

3 _____

_____

4 _____

_____

5 _____

_____

6 _____

_____

7 _____

_____

8 _____

_____

9 _____

_____

10 _____

_____

The name of my album is...

_____

_____

_____

_____

I chose this title because it represents...

_____

_____

_____

_____

_____

_____

My favorite track is(why?)

My least favorite track is (why?)

Today's topic: PLACES TO GO & PEOPLE TO SEE. Take some time to think about where you are in your life? Are you working to fulfill your goals, dreams, destiny? Name at least three places you would like to visit and name three people who you would like to visit these places with. What is it going to take for you to make this goal happen?

The places I am going to visit are:

1_____

_____

2_____

_____

3_____

_____

These are the people i would like to have as a traveling companion (why)?

_____

_____

_____

_____

_____

INSPIRATIONAL HAIKU

A traditional Japanese haiku is a three lined poem with seventeen syllables, written in a 5/7/5 syllable count. It focuses on images from nature and emphasizes simplicity, intensity, and directness of expression. Here is my example of an inspirational haiku:

GOD'S GRACE AND MERCY

HAS BROUGHT LOVE, PEACE, CLARITY

THAT IS JOY EVERYDAY!

After reading it a few times, challenge yourself to create a haiku about something that inspires you. Incorporate your hopes, dreams, or simply think about the most important thing you can imagine in life and open your creative writing skills.

_____

_____

_____

ALWAYS REMEMBER THERE IS NOTHING YOU CAN DO THAT CAN'T BE DONE!

You have come to the end of your workbook and journal! Congratulations for staying the course and practicing the skills of speaking positivity into your life!

It is our hope and prayer that this has been a life altering journey that you will continue beyond the pages in this book and that you will periodically go back and reflect on your writing!

Sincerely,
Sherry Sheffield, MA, LPC, LADC
Robin Turner, MS, LMFT-I, CADC-I

The End